I0201374

The Hub

12 Secrets to Answered Prayer

Dalen Garris

This is a work of history. Historical individuals and places and events are mentioned.

Copyright © 2023 by Dalen Garris

Published by Revivalfire Ministries

ISBN 13: 979-8-9894310-0-7

All rights reserved.
No part of this book may be used or reproduced in any manner whatsoever, without written permission, except in the case of brief quotations embodied in critical articles and reviews, as provided by U.S. Copyright Law.

For information, address
dale@revivalfire.org

First paperback printing November, 2023

Printed in the United States of America

Introduction

Everyone wants God to pay attention to them. So, we pray with the hope that God will actually hear us and answer us. But what are the rules for getting those prayers not just heard, but answered?

There are many books written on the secret to prayer. We are given advice on how to pray, how long to pray, how loud to pray, where to pray, what mindset we should have when we pray, what scriptures to read before we pray, and who we should pray with. I'm sure that's all good advice, but what I want to know is, not how to pray, but how to get answers to prayer.

Plenty of scriptures admonish us to have faith so we can move mountains, but I believe that there are conditions that God requires of us to validate that faith to get it moving. Understand those conditions, and you can unlock the promises.

We are dealing with an invisible world for which we are given a book of clues. As with everything in God, the answers are in His Word, and it will all seem so simple when we finally cross over and see Him face-to-face, but for now, we must follow that which is revealed in His Word.

Each of these secrets taken separately is like a spoke on a wheel. None are sufficient alone but need the support of all the others to make a fully functional wheel. Some may seem repetitious, but each passage brings its own nuances. The Word of God will weave a tapestry that will reveal His face when it is finally woven together.

I started with nine secrets. Then there were ten, then twelve . . . you know how it goes with each new revelation that God shows you. Finally, I came to realize that there is only one master secret for all prayer from all people. It is the hub for all the different spokes. I will reserve that for last, but I'm telling you about it now, so you won't quit reading until you reach it.

If there was ever a time that we needed prayer warriors who can contend to the Throne of God, it is now. We are about to enter an age of unbelievably intense spiritual warfare. Satan is loosed upon the earth, the powers of darkness are growing, and the spirit of Antichrist is rising out of the sea. Prayer is our weapon, but we need champions of the faith to wield that weapon victoriously.

I am praying that warrior is you.

Let's start with the first one – faith.

Faith

Mark 11:22-25 – And Jesus answering saith unto them, Have faith in God.

For verily I say unto you, That whosoever shall say unto this mountain, Be thou removed, and be thou cast into the sea; and shall not doubt in his heart, but shall believe that those things which he saith shall come to pass; he shall have whatsoever he saith.

Therefore, I say unto you, What things soever ye desire, when ye pray, believe that ye receive them, and ye shall have them.

1 John 5:15 – And if we know that he hear us, whatsoever we ask, we know that we have the petitions that we desired of him.

You have to believe God. Simple as that. Or is it? How many times have we heard of having the childlike faith to trust our Heavenly Father to take care of us? And yet, it's not quite that simple, is it? We can't just snap our fingers and expect God to leap into action, deliver us from our troubles, and set us on high. There's something more to it than that.

God wants to be believed above all things, and without faith, it's impossible to please Him. (Heb. 11:6). Abraham was called the Friend of God because he believed God in spite of his circumstances. There was an acknowledgment that God was more real than the physical world around him. Joshua believed that so much that he called for the sun to stop . . . and it did. Chapter 11 of Hebrews is called the Hall of Heroes because of those who chose to have faith in that which they could not see rather than their physical circumstance that they could see.

But faith alone doesn't always get us the results we were asking for, and neither does it always deliver us from the horrors that we face. That is when faith must merge with trust that He has a plan, and we are part of that plan. It may not be what we hoped for, but we are part of a greater reality that includes us as an integral part of that plan.

What if God told you of someone down in the bottom of some dungeon who, if someone would just go down there to witness to him, would become another great John the Baptist? If He asked you to please go, would you do it? Of course, you would. The thing is, He doesn't ask you. He just sends you, and you wind up in the bottom of a dungeon wondering what happened. Do you still trust Him? Do you still have a hold on your faith? That is how faith and trust merge.

Faith sets the stage for prayer. It may not be the final answer to your prayers, but nothing works without it. Faith is where it starts. It is the ocean on which our ship sails. Amongst all the other secrets of answered prayer, faith must come first. All the others are built upon that foundation.

Sincerity

"My little children, let us not love in word, neither in tongue; but in deed and in truth. And hereby we know that we are of the truth, and shall assure our hearts before him." (1 John 3:18, 19)

John tells us not to love in word, but in deed and in truth. In other words, talk is cheap. Many people profess that they believe in God and even show up for church, but if your sincerity stops at the church door, then your faith is a little short. The love of God is not something we feel but something we do. Sunday Christians need not apply. If you are not serious, why would you expect God to be serious?

Sincerity is not a quality of the brain; it is something that is in your heart. It drives you straight through difficult times, holds on long after desire has let go, and determines the depth of your character.

How sincere are you when you say you love? Do you really mean it, or do you only love when it is something you like? Are you willing to put works to your faith, even when it is hard? Do you believe even when it is inconvenient? If your sincerity in prayer is not enough to raise your prayers past the ceiling, they will not reach the Throne of God.

John tells us that we will know if we are of the truth by our sincerity (1st John 3:19). We assure our hearts before God when we know that we are not phony but are willing to give our all to what we believe. It will show up in our prayers and our confidence before God.

The sincerity of your prayers will evoke a reciprocal response from God.

Power of Praise

Enter into his gates with thanksgiving, and into his courts with praise: be thankful unto him and bless his name. (Psalms 100:4)

As a young Christian, I was taught to always start my prayer hours by praising and thanking the Lord. Sometimes it would take 5, 10, 15 minutes, but rarely did the Lord not answer and bless me with His Spirit. Yeah, there were times when it seemed hard, but when I started with praise, it always lubricated my time of prayer.

Why is that? I don't know. Maybe because God loves praise. Maybe the power of praise is just that simple. If you want His attention, come with thanksgiving and praise, and watch how He responds.

David's Worship

There is no overestimating the power of praise. David was the apple of God's eye because he knew how to worship. He loved God with all his heart, and Psalms is the outpouring of his heart full of praise toward his God.

What was David's doctrine? What did he believe or not believe? Nobody knows. What about his righteousness? What about all the sins he committed and the mistakes that he made? All of that was overshadowed by David's enormous outpouring of praise of God. God loved David because David loved God, and as a result, he found enormous Grace and favor with God.

The Alabaster Box

We see another example of the power of praise in the fragrance from the precious ointment that was released when Mary broke the alabaster box. That alabaster box was a picture of Mary's heart that was broken for her Savior. John chapter 12 says that the fragrance of that praise filled the room. Praise has that effect. It fills the room as your prayers ascend to the Throne of God. The carnal is replaced with the spiritual as the doors to the courts open, and you step into the Presence of God.

The others did not understand, but Mary, who had no theological background or any religious mindset, did not have to know. She just worshipped Jesus, and that was enough to memorialize her for the ages to come.

Mary is a unique character in her simplicity, her faith, and her worship of her Savior. There cannot be any question of the depth of devotion and praise this woman had for Jesus. When all had fled, Mary lingered at the tomb, searching for where they had taken her Lord. Even in death, He was still her Lord.

And then she heard His voice, "Mary". One more time, even before He had ascended to Heaven to apply His blood to the real altar in Heaven, He risked all just to hear her worship one more time. He could not allow her to touch Him yet, or He would have been defiled, but oh, to receive that worship one more time.

That's the power of praise.

Psalm 91

He that dwelleth in the secret place of the Most High shall abide under the shadow of the Almighty.

I will say of the Lord, He is my refuge and my fortress: my God; in him will I trust.

Because thou hast made the Lord, which is my refuge, even the Most High, thy habitation; There shall no evil befall thee, neither shall any plague come nigh thy dwelling.

He shall call upon me, and I will answer him:

(Psalms 91: 1, 2, 14, 15)

The modern grace-orientated gospel of prosperity offers blessings without price, but this Psalm calls for a dwelling and a refuge in a secret place in God where you can abide under His shadow. This is a place of prayer where you pour yourself out before Him. Your cries must come out of knowing the crucified and broken depths of the suffering of the Body of Christ. That suffering opens the depths of our hearts, enables a true love within us for the lost, and gives us compassion for the pain that sin causes. It brings passion to your prayers and strength to your faith that you will only find in that secret place of the Most High.

Do you really know Him in the sufferings of the Cross? Are you in that secret place? Is He your soul's habitation?

All that is easy to say, but that kind of depth requires a submersion into Him that obscures the world and everything in it. He has to be the air you breathe, the thoughts you think, and the nourishment your soul feeds on. You dive into the waters of His presence and swim in the waters of His love. The world and the flesh fade into the background and no longer affect you. You are in that secret place of the Most High.

It is not an easy place to get to. It takes a constant effort to subdue the carnal because the flesh wars against the spirit (Gal. 5:17). But it is worth every effort because once you enter that grace, you are set free, and your communion with your Creator gives your prayers free access to the Throne of God.

The Effect of Sin on Prayer

Victory comes when we abstain from sin. When we give into temptation, we relinquish our grip on righteousness and lose our hold on that victory.

Sin destroys answered prayer. I hear many claim that because our flesh is corrupt, we cannot help but sin every day, and therefore, we cannot walk uprightly in God. I don't believe that. It is one thing to say that we all make mistakes, slip, and fall occasionally, but it is another thing to shift the blame to our sinful flesh and call for Grace as a covering. You cannot minimize sin just because we are under Grace. Grace is not a covering or an excuse for sin; it is the power that God gives us to overcome sin. That overcoming power over sin is what gives us the victory to claim answers to prayer.

To say otherwise allows Satan to steal our victory before we even try. We cannot blame our flesh for our failures any more than Adam could blame Eve for his. The whole point of the new covenant was that the Spirit of God would be inside us so we would overcome sin (Jer. 31:33). Jesus died on the Cross to deliver us from sin, not give us a free covering. If we sin, we break that fellowship with God and lose our access to answered prayer.

Let me offer some scriptures to back that up:

Psalms 66:18 - *If I regard iniquity in my heart, the Lord will not hear me:*

John 9:31 - *Now we know that God heareth not sinners: but if* any man be a worshipper of God, and doeth his will, him he heareth.

Micah 3:4 - *Then shall they cry unto the LORD, but he will not hear them: he will even hide his face from them at that time, as they have behaved themselves ill in their doings.*

Proverbs 28:9 - *He that turneth away his ear from hearing the law, even his prayer shall be abomination.*

Proverbs 15:29 - *The LORD is far from the wicked: but he heareth the prayer of the righteous.*

 Zechariah 7:13 - *Therefore it is come to pass, that as he cried, and they would not hear; so they cried, and I would not hear, saith the LORD of hosts:*

Isaiah 59:2 - *But your iniquities have separated between you and your God, and your sins have hid his face from you, that he will not hear.*

1John 3:22 - *And whatsoever we ask, we receive of him, because we keep his commandments, and do those things that are pleasing in his sight.*

Proverbs 1:24-29 - *Because I have called, and ye refused; I have stretched out my hand, and no man regarded; But ye have set at nought all my counsel, and would none of my reproof: I also will laugh at your calamity; I will mock when your fear cometh; When your fear cometh as desolation, and your destruction cometh as a whirlwind; when distress and anguish cometh upon you. Then shall they call upon me, but I will not answer; they shall seek me early, but they shall not find me:*

For that they hated knowledge, and did not choose the fear of the LORD:

Sin destroys your relationship with God, but righteousness gives you victory, confidence, and holy boldness to step in before the Throne of God. Righteousness establishes the promises of God and gives you the faith to receive the promises you have claimed.

They will not come without it.

Holy Boldness through Righteousness

*For if our heart condemn us, God is greater than our heart, and knoweth all things. Beloved, if our heart condemn us not, then have we confidence toward God. And **whatsoever we ask, we receive of him, because we keep his commandments, and do those things that are pleasing in his sight**. (1 John 3: 18-22)*

Holy Boldness. It is the Breakfast of Champions. To have such confidence in God that you are not afraid to walk right into the Holy of Holies and stand before God in prayer! That's the kind of faith in God that takes authority over the weak and beggarly elements of the world and wins victories.

Where does such confidence come from? Righteousness and the fear of God.

God is a righteous God, and His core personality is holiness. It may be said that the love of God and the fear of God both emanate from that holiness. He requires us to walk in that same righteousness. That was the very purpose of the New Covenant - to allow us to take on the very nature of God and have the power to walk in righteousness (Jer. 31:31-35). Jesus gave His life so we could have the power to overcome sin and walk in the boldness of righteousness.

Sin, however, separates us from God (Isaiah 59:2) and undermines our stance with Him. We can feel the separation as we are no longer walking in the same steps as He is. Our prayers no longer find traction, and our guilt lies heavy on us. Victory slips out of our grasp.

God sends us Holy Ghost conviction as a gift to lead us to repentance so that we can be freed from sin's power, but it is always our choice whether or not to avail ourselves of that gift. If we do not, our hearts will condemn us because we know we are in sin. And we know that God also knows, and that hampers our confidence in prayer.

But, if we walk in righteousness as He walks, then we have that confidence to stand before Him in holy boldness to claim the promises of God (1 John 1:7). If sin is no longer a part of our lives, then the separation it brings is gone, and we stand face-to-face with our Savior without the veil of shame or the weight of guilt. We now have a righteous claim to the promises of God.

All the promises of God come with conditions. If you do this, then God will do that. I know of no promises that are not like that. If you want God to do what you want, then you have to do what He wants, and His Word to us is to keep His commandments.

I have often said that righteousness establishes the promises of God. When you are keeping the commandments of God, you know you are righteous, and there is a boldness and confidence that accompanies it that opens the heavens to you. You have kept His Word, and so He has to keep His Word to you.

What a feeling of victory that is to know that you are right with your God! And so now, whatsoever you ask – did you catch that? Whatsoever! – we receive of Him. Why? Because we keep His commandments AND do the things that are pleasing unto Him.

When you keep His commandments, you are righteous, and you fulfill the covenant made with Him, and so you, therefore, inherit the promises. But there is a second part to that equation – to do the things that are pleasing to Him. This brings us back to love.

Love is the keeping of God's commandments. Jesus said in John 14:15 if you love me, keep my commandments, and again in John 15:10 that if you keep His commandments, you will abide in His love. But full love is more than strict, cold-hearted righteousness. There is something more to love than mindless obedience to the laws of God. The Pharisees were squeaky clean, and yet they're burning in Hell.

I have always felt that the old King James' translation of the word "agape" to "charity" was much better than the newer versions of "love" because love can be thought of as a warm fuzzy emotion, but charity is love in action. It is like a faith validated by works. It is defined by what it does rather than what it feels like. Love is the flesh on the skeleton of righteousness that fills out the Body of Christ. Love without righteousness cannot stand by itself; righteousness without love is a bunch of dead bones.

When you are walking in the kind of righteousness

manifested in God's love, you will manifest a genuine love for the brethren and lost souls. This is what is pleasing in His sight.

And when you have that, you can stand before God and claim your answers to prayer.

Winning the Lost – John 15

I am the vine, ye are the branches: He that abideth in me, and I in him, the same bringeth forth much fruit: for without me ye can do nothing.

If a man abide not in me, he is cast forth as a branch, and is withered; and men gather them, and cast them into the fire, and they are burned. If ye abide in me, and my words abide in you, **ye shall ask what ye will, and it shall be done unto you.**

Herein is my Father glorified, that ye bear much fruit; so shall ye be my disciples.

Ye have not chosen me, but I have chosen you, and ordained you, that ye should go and bring forth fruit, and that your fruit should remain: that whatsoever ye shall ask of the Father in my name, he may give it you." (John 15: 5-8, 16)

When preaching about revival, the focus is always on winning the lost. It is the primary reason Jesus came and died, and it is what He has called the Church to carry on in His absence. It was His last request just before He ascended into the heavens. If there is one function of the Church that is more important than all others, it is to win souls.

If we want God to move for us, then it stands to reason that we need to do what He has asked us to do. I often joke that God is a Jewish businessman – He makes deals. You do this, and He will do that. Every promise of

God has a contingency. If we want Him to move for us, we need to do what He asks. So, what has He asked us to do? Simple. Go win souls. "Go into all the world ...." (Mark 16:15)

Parable of the True Vine

The Parable of the True Vine brings up four important points that God requires in our deal for answered prayer. The first is that we must abide in Him, and He in us to bring forth fruit. Just like sap in a tree, the Spirit of God must flow through us in order to produce fruit for the harvest. It is the Lord, not us, who will draw all men unto Him. (John 12:32) Without Jesus in us, we can do nothing (John 15:5). This is **what** we have to do.

The second point in this parable to understand is that if we abide in Him and His words abide in us, we can ask what we will, and it will be done for us (John 15:7). In order for the Word to abide in us, we have to read it, not just superficially, but we must let His words find a place of habitation in us. It has to take over our lives and be the air we breathe. In Philippians 2:13, Paul writes that God will work in us to give us the will, desire, and power to do His will. But for that to happen, the Word has to abide in the very depth of our hearts. That is **how** we do it.

The third point that John 15 hammers home is that winning souls glorifies the Father. To glorify God is the ultimate purpose of our salvation. And then, just to drive the point home, he reminds us that this is how we become His disciples. Winning souls is that important, not only to those who get saved but to us if we want to continue as His disciples. The overtones are severe. This is **why** we do it.

The fourth point is that we were ordained, not just called, to not only win souls, but to keep them. This is the condition for the promise that He then offers us that whatever we ask the Father, He may give it to us. This is **what** we receive when we do it.

To Love Souls is the fullness of praise

How do we bring ourselves to a fullness of worship and praise? To be able to truly praise God, you have to love God. That's what praise is – the love of God manifested in our lips, our hearts, and our actions. According to 1st John, to love God, you have to love souls.

> *"Everyone who loves Him that begat loves Him also who is begotten of Him."* (1 John 5:1)

That's the condition. God is all about winning the lost – He gave His life for them -- so you have to be about the same. But, to love souls, you have to get rid of your pride. Jesus told us plainly in Luke 9:24 that if any man will come after Him, he has to lose his life. The Gospel is not about you; it's about others. You have to take the focus off yourself. The fear of the Lord will do that for you. It is an eradicator of pride and arrogance (Prov. 8:13).

According to James1:5, to get wisdom, you have to ask. And according to Jobe 28:28, wisdom is the fear of the Lord, so it stands to reason that to receive the fear of the

Lord, we have to ask for it.

To sum this all up, in order to enter into a depth of worship and praise so that your prayers can be heard, you must:

1. Praise Him sincerely.
2. To praise Him, you must love Him.
3. To love God, you must love souls (1 John 5:1)
4. To love souls, you must get rid of pride (Luke 9:23, 24)
5. To get rid of pride, you must have the fear of God.
6. To get fear, you have to ask in prayer (James 1:5)
7. To get the power to pray, you must read the Word of God.

Simple.

The Power of the Word of God

I believe that the source of the power to pray at a level of desperation and passion can only come from the Word of God. There is a power in the Word that affects and anoints you when you yield to it and allow God to use you. Philippians 2:13 tells us that God will work in us to give us the power and the will to serve Him. How does God get inside you so He can work? By reading His Word.

Prov. 26:20 tells us that where no wood is, there the fire goes out. If the fire is the Holy Spirit, then the wood is the Word of God. The Word has to be in place for the Spirit to light it.

The Word of God gives us sustenance (Bread of Life), vision (Light of the World), a reason to care (Great Commission), and passion (will).

It also gives us faith, and faith moves mountains.

If we want to access the overcoming prayer life that we need, we will need the fire from the Altar of God in Heaven. How do we get all the way up there to get that fire? It starts with faith.

Without faith, Hebrews 11:6 tells us, it is impossible to please God. It would be senseless to start praying if you didn't believe He will hear you, never mind answer you. Before we start battling our way up to God in prayer, we need a healthy dose of faith to energize our prayers.

Where do we get that faith from? Faith comes by

hearing, and hearing by the Word of God (Rom 10:17).

1st John 5:7 tells us that the Spirit and the Word are one and agree together. That tells us that:

1. When we read God's Word, we hear His voice, and that gives us a certain measure of faith.
2. When we take that faith into the prayer room, it will take us up in the Spirit.
3. Since God dwells in the praises and thanks of His saints, when your faith brings you up, the Spirit will come down.
4. When you take that Spirit you just received in the prayer room back to the Word of God, you will go deeper. What happens when you go deeper into the Word of God? You get more faith.
5. Take that faith back to the prayer room, and you will go higher,
6. then deeper, and higher, and deeper and higher until the friction ignites a fire in your heart that cannot be put out.

I know of no other way to light that fire. Everything in God comes down to reading and prayer.

Water Represents the Word of God

There are a couple of other passages that I use when I preach revival that use water as a symbol of the Word of God – Elijah on Mt. Carmel and Jesus at Cana of Galilee.

Water, throughout the Bible, symbolizes the Word of God. For instance, Ephesians calls for the "washing of the water of the Word." Moses struck the Rock (Jesus, the

Word of God), and out came water. The Laver of Brass in the Tabernacle held water for the priests to wash with before they ministered. In Exodus 38:8, we are told that the brass for the laver came from the mirrors of the women in the congregation. Why did God put that in Scripture? Because, when you looked into the water of the Word of God in the laver of brass, you would see the reflection of your heart and wash in the water of the Word of God before you went to minister. So, water represents the Word of God.

Elijah on Mt. Carmel

In 1st Kings chapter 17, Israel was in a drought, both spiritually and physically. Elijah called for a sacrifice on Mt. Carmel to challenge the priests of Baal. This would be a test to see which god would pour down fire from heaven on the sacrifice.

The priests of Baal went first, calling upon their god all day long. When Baal didn't answer, it was Elijah's turn. He rebuilt the altar and laid the sacrifice and the wood on it. But before Elijah called upon God, he first called for twelve barrels of water and drenched both the sacrifice and the altar. Why was that?

But, there was no place to get the water because of the drought. All the rivers were dried up. And they were on the top of a mountain! To get water, they had to go all the way down to the ocean at the bottom of Mt. Carmel to get the water and drag it back up the mountain. Elijah then poured those twelve barrels of water on the sacrifice. It did not matter how hard it was to get that water. There could be no excuses because Elijah knew that the fire of God would not fall on the sacrifice until it was drenched with the water of the Word of God. If you want the fire of God to fall on your sacrifice, you will have to do the same.

Cana of Galilee

Another example of the power of the Word of God is at the wedding in Cana in the 2nd chapter of John. They had a problem because there was no wine at the wedding. Since wine often symbolizes the Spirit of God and the Church is the Bride of Christ, then it can be said that a wedding without wine is like a church without the Spirit.

What was Jesus' solution? There were six waterpots of clay. Six is the number that represents Man, and the Bible refers to us as vessels of clay, so it may be said that those six waterpots represent the people in the church. Fill the waterpots with water. How high? To the brim! Why? Because when you are filled to the brim with the Word of God, something miraculous happens. The Spirit and the Word agree (1John 5:8), and the water turns to wine! That is the power of the Word of God.

God's Word is the source of all nourishment, faith, power, and passion. It has to be the window through which we view the world. The road to the Throne of God leads through His Word, and your faith, passion, zeal, power and vision are all fueled by it.

Jesus said that without Him, we can do nothing. (John 15:5), and He was the Word of God.

Isaiah 58 - Having mercy on the lost.

In Isaiah 58, we hear the cry of those who believe they are in the Lord but are not getting any response from Him. Jerusalem is symbolic of the Church, so we can apply this passage to our churches of today.

> *"Wherefore have we fasted, say they, and thou seest not? Wherefore have we afflicted our soul, and thou takest no knowledge?" (Isa. 58:3)*

What's wrong? What are we missing? We pray, we fast, but God is not answering. There's a little bit here and a little bit over there, but the fullness of the Spirit that we have been promised has not manifested itself fully in our churches today. Much like in Amos chapter 4 where it rains a little bit in one city and then a little bit in another, but never enough to cure the drought. So it is today with our drought of revival.

The following nine verses are God's answer:

If you do this (verses 6, 7):

- Loose the bands of wickedness
- Undo heavy burdens of sin
- Let the oppressed go free from sin
- Break every yoke of sin
- Share your bread (the Bread of Life) with the hungry
- Bring them into your house, the House of God
- Cover the naked with robes of righteousness

Then God will do this (verse 8):

- Your Light will break forth like the morning
- Your healing will spring forth speedily
- Your righteousness will go before you
- The glory of the Lord will be your rear reward

If you (verse 10):

- draw out your soul to those who are hungry for God, and
- satisfy the soul that is afflicted with sin

Then, (verse 10,11):

- Your light will rise in obscurity
- The Lord will guide you continually.
- He will satisfy your soul in drought, spiritual drought

And best of all, in verse 9:

Then shalt thou call, and the LORD shall answer; thou shalt cry, and he shall say, Here I am."

The secret to having God answer you, therefore, is contingent upon having mercy on lost souls. Mercy begets mercy. (Matt. 5:7)

There is one more verse that I would point to as the culminating point of this passage:

You will build the old waste places, raise up the foundations that were broken down, be called the

Repairer of the Breach, the Restorer of paths to dwell in. (Isaiah 58:12)

If Jerusalem is a picture of the Church, then the Babylonians' destruction and judgment of Jerusalem would speak of the apostasy the Church has fallen into, especially in these last days. Plenty of passages in the Word of God support the idea that there would be a great apostasy just before the Day of the Lord.

If that is the case, then the prophecies of a great revival at the end must also be true. This generation will build the old waste places of the Church that once were alive and vibrant in the Holy Spirit. We will raise up the foundations that the Church was built on, just like Nehemiah did. This army of on-fire born-again believers like those we see in Joel chapter 2 will rise up to declare victory in Jesus Christ, and they will forever be called the Repairers of the Breach, the Restorers of the Old Paths (Jer. 6:16).

How will this be possible? Those who will show mercy on the lost will be able to rebuild the old foundations and restore the paths to walk in. They will usher in the last, great revival just before Jesus Christ splits the eastern skies.

If you want to be part of this great, victorious army, then the instructions are laid out for you. In its distilled essence:

Go win souls.

Persistence in Prayer

Col. 4:2 – Continue in prayer, and watch in the same with thanksgiving;"

The old-timers used to pray for hours, even all night, if needed. They didn't pray until they were tired; they prayed until they got an answer. They called it "praying it through". I can still remember the admonishment from my pastor that many Christians will pray until they feel the winds of victory begin to blow across their face and then quit just before the finish line. She would command us that instead we should keep on praying until we had a firm grasp on a full answer from God. Don't quit until you have the victory! Don't back down. Stand faith-believing that God will answer. And don't move until He does!

Faith isn't believing that God can do anything. Any fool can believe that. Faith is believing that He <u>will</u> do it, and you will stand in contending prayer until He does. That is true faith.

But we do not see that kind of prayer these days. Maybe because the price is too high. Maybe we don't care that much. Maybe we have lost our grip on that level of faith. Or maybe we have never heard about that kind of fierce, contending warfare, and we simply don't know how to pray like that. Whatever the reason, we have lost something essential to our Christian faith.

Consider this quote from Peggy Smith, one of the old women who birthed the Hebrides Revival. This is coming from two old women, 82 and 84 years old, one crippled and the other blind, who refused to back down until they saw God move.

> "We struggled through the hours of the night, refusing to take a denial. Had He not promised? And would He not fulfill? Our God is a covenant-keeping God, and he must be true to His covenant arrangement.

> Did He fail us? Never! Before the morning broke, we saw the enemy retreating, and our wonderful Lamb take the field.

> We had a consciousness of God that created a confidence in our souls which refused to accept defeat."

How bad do you want an answer? Are you willing to fight for it? Will you keep on praying until you gain victory? Do you have enough faith to believe that if you keep praying that God will answer? Are you willing to cry out to God with force and passion until He does?

In Luke 18:8, Jesus tells us to pray like the women before the unjust judge. She would not let up until it drove him crazy. He granted her petition just to shut her up!

In Genesis 32:22-30, Jacob wrestled with the Angel and refused to let go until the Angel blessed him. He fought all night long, but that's what prayer warriors do. You fight until you win.

Elijah had just called down fire out of heaven. He had stopped the heavens from rain for 3½ years. When he walked into a room, he brought in with him the presence of authority in God and stood down kings and priests. "The Lord God", he said, "before Whom I stand." He literally stood before the presence of God Almighty. And yet, he had to pray seven times before he saw the promise of rain on the horizon.

In Deuteronomy 9:25, Moses had to pray for forty days and nights to save the children of Israel from God's determined wrath.

Both Daniel and David prayed three times a day. They were in charge of empires, but they found the time to pray. How much more do we have to continue to contend in prayer before God if we want the same results? There are times when you just simply have to get an answer from God, so you stay there until he answers.

Psalms 55:16 – As for me, I will call upon God; and the LORD shall save me.

Do you believe that? If you really believe that, will you keep going until you get an answer?

Old-fashioned prayer warriors prayed all night long. Kings prayed three times a day. Prophets contended until the rain fell. Widows hammered away until they were heard. Prayer moves God. If you want God to move, you will have to pray until He does.

Heb. 6:15 - And so, after he had patiently endured, he obtained the promise

Passionate desperate prayer

"… The effectual fervent prayer of a righteous man avails much. Elias was a man subject to like passions as we are, and he prayed earnestly that it might not rain: and it rained not on the earth by the space of three years and six months." (James 5:16-17)

"And from the days of John the Baptist until now the kingdom of heaven suffers violence, and the violent take it by force." (Matthew 11:12)

Prayer is the art of war, and the Prayer Room is our battlefield. While it may be wonderful to have those times of intimate, quiet communion with God, we are nevertheless called to war. Prayer, fueled by the faith that comes from the Word of God, is our weapon. Satan fears nothing more than a prayer warrior who has the persistence to fight for the things of God.

Jesus said that the kingdom of Heaven suffers violence, and the violent take it by force (Matt. 11:12). Does that sound like a soft, "quiet time with Jesus"? There are times for soft, intimate prayers, but if you are called to the battle, then you will have to pick up your sword and charge into the battle of prayer. You will have to cry out to God with force and passion.

Where do we get passion like that to ignite a fury of Holy Ghost fire that will win souls, birth revivals, raise the dead, and turn a society inside out with the fire of God? It doesn't come by wishful thinking or having a "little talk with Jesus." The fire we need can only be found on the true Altar in Heaven. That's the true source of all holy fire.

To get that fire, it takes a desperate effort of fierce prayer to reach all the way up to the Altar of God and bring it down. The old-timers called it "storming the Throne of God." They contended before God, not until they were tired, but until they had the victory.

> *And from the days of John the Baptist until now the kingdom of heaven suffereth violence, and the violent take it by force. (Matthew 11:12)*

Passion has a price. It is difficult these days to find those who are willing to pray that hard. Perhaps that is why we find so many of today's churches anemic and powerless. If we want God to hear us, we have to have the passion of desperate prayer to reach Him. Leonard Ravenhill wrote that God doesn't answer prayer; He answers desperate prayer!

Consider the prophet Jonah. Running from God, Jonah found himself in the belly of a whale with no hope of getting out. But Jonah knew if he could reach God with enough desperation, God would hear and pardon him. I doubt if anyone prayed with more passionate desperation.

> *Then I said, I am cast out of thy sight; yet I will look again toward thy holy temple.*
>
> *When my soul fainted within me, I remembered the LORD: and my prayer came in unto thee, into thine*

holy temple. They that observe lying vanities forsake their own mercy. (Jonah 2:4,7-8)

The power of that desperate prayer was so great that it the whale committed suicide just so Jonah wouldn't get his feet wet.

That's the power of passionate, desperate prayer.

The Hub of the Wheel

And so, we come to the final secret: the Hub that all the spokes fit into. All the secrets that we have discussed above are all true. Each one is essential in its own way. Each has a condition that God has put before us that opens the door for prayer to be answered. But why don't they work all the time?

A Christian chiropractor here in Texas was asked by his young daughter why God doesn't answer our prayers right away? He said he had to think about that for a moment, but then he answered that if God answered all our prayers right away, we wouldn't realize how much we need Him.

I've thought about that over the years when faced with the same question from those in desperate need. Some theologians might argue the point, but I think there is something essential in that answer. God is sovereign. Never forget that. Ask Job. He is God and the Creator of all things, and there is a purpose to every single element of this reality that He has created.

You may not know or understand what is happening around you or why the things happening to you do not make sense. God told us to believe, and you believed, but your prayers were still not answered. Why?

Like spokes on a wheel, each of the secrets we discussed have two ends. One extends out into the Wheel of Life, supporting its individual portion of the wheel. The other end is inserted into the Hub, the heart of the entire wheel where our desires merge with His and where we allow Him to work in us to do His Will, not ours. When our prayers, our desires, and the cries of our hearts yield to the Will of God, we finally come into complete agreement with Him, and our prayers merge with His in the Hub of the Wheel of Life.

This is a place of complete and final trust. Our lives are no longer about us and what we want. Our trust in God is no longer linked to a Prosperity message about the blessings that are coming to our lives and what we can get from God, but now becomes a surrender to His Will and a trust that, whatever part we are called to play in His plan, whether it is good or not, we trust Him. We may be called to sickness, captivity, or pain. We may find ourselves in relative obscurity while others seem to prosper in everything they do. We may see others take the credit for what we have done, while we receive the scorn of the world. Or like Job, watch everything we cherish in this life be destroyed for no apparent reason. And yet, we trust in the Living God that He not only knows what we are going through, but is allowing us to go through our tribulation on purpose because, ultimately, He has a plan, and we are part of that plan. We trust Him, and so submit to His Will and into the perfect peace of God that passes all understanding.

It is about God's Will and what He wants. Our desires merge with the Cross in the Hub of Prayer as we deny ourselves, pick up our cross, and follow Him. At that point, we die out to our own will and enter into His Rest.

And the Wheel turns.

About the Author

Dalen Garris has been in ministry since 1970 during the Jesus Movement in California. In 1997, he began a radio broadcast that ultimately spread to dozens of countries, from Israel and Saudi Arabia to Africa and the Philippines. His program, *Fire in the Hole*, was selected for broadcast across North America on the Sky Angel network as the Voice of Jerusalem.

A newspaper column followed, for which he has written over 700 articles, which have been published in local newspapers and Christian magazines in several countries. He has also written over a dozen books and several booklets.

Since 2004, he has been lighting the fires of revival in churches spread across sub-Saharan Africa. During the course of 17 years, he has preached in over 1,000 churches and has seen hundreds of them set on fire and explode with growth, and hundreds of new ones planted across Africa. Hundreds of people have been supernaturally healed during the healing lines that so often sprang up during these revival meetings, and tens of thousands have been saved. And the fires are still burning.

Because of his work across Africa, Dalen Garris was awarded an honorary Doctorate in 2017 by the Northwestern Christian University of Florida. He was also awarded the Brevet de Merite from the Vision Barza Grands Lacs coalition of churches.

Dr. Garris currently lives with Cindy, his wife of 45 years, in Waxahachie and is still heavily involved with churches across Africa. His pressing hope is in seeing this powerful move of God in Africa ignite us here in America. He believes that this upcoming generation will be the Gideon Generation that will usher in this last, great revival that he has preached about for so many years.

If you would like Dalen Garris to speak at your church or organization, please contact us for times and schedules. We do not charge, nor will we ever charge, to preach the Gospel anywhere in the world.

Books by Dalen Garris:

Available at: www.Revivalfre.org/books

Four Steps to Revival

Do You Have Eternal Security?

Standing in the Gap – Test of a True Prophet

Two Covenants – Torah-based Faith vs. Grace

The Hub – 12 Secrets to Answered Prayer

Fire in the Hole

Revival Campaigns

The Kenya Diaries

A Trumpet in Nigeria

A Scent of Rain

Into the Heart of Darkness

Fire and Rain

Revival Campaigns in Africa – 2019

The Battle for Nigeria

 A Light in the Bush

A Match in Dry Grass

Planting a Seed in Liberia

A Whisper in the Wind

Talking With the Women, by Cindy

Tanzania, A Rumbling Under the Mountain

A Voice in the Wilderness:

vol. 1, The Journey Begins

vol. 2, the Early Years

vol. 3, Prophet Rising

vol. 4, Revival in the Wings

vol. 5, Sound of an Abundance of Rain

vol. 6, Watchman, What of the Night?

vol. 7, Mud and Heroes

vol. 8, Ashes in the Morning

vol. 9, Shaking the Olive Tree

vol. 10, Winds of Change

vol. 11, A Final Call

vol. 12, Superficial Shells

Booklets

Available at: www.Revivalfire.org/booklets/

A Volcano in Cape Verde

Nigeria, 2012

Calvinism Critique

RevivalFire Ministries

PO Box 822
Waxahachie, TX 75168
dale@revivalfire.org

www.ingramcontent.com/pod-product-compliance
Lightning Source LLC
Chambersburg PA
CBHW071747020426
42331CB00008B/2206